THE TEN: 6–10

—

WRITTEN BY JEFF PRIES

THOMAS NELSON
Since 1798

NASHVILLE DALLAS MEXICO CITY RIO DE JANEIRO BEIJING

Published in Nashville, Tennessee, by Thomas Nelson. Thomas Nelson is a registered trademark of Thomas Nelson, Inc.

Published in association with the literary agency of Yates & Yates, LLP, Attorneys and Counselors, Orange, California.

Thomas Nelson, Inc. titles may be purchased in bulk for educational, business, fund-raising, or sales promotional use. For information, please e-mail SpecialMarkets@ThomasNelson.com.

ISBN 978-1-4185-3417-2

Printed in China.
09 10 11 12 13 SF 6 5 4 3 2 1

■ CONTENTS

■ INTRODUCTION

LIQUID

Five episodes. One story.

God's Word is as true today as it was when it was written.

But for too long, we have looked at God's Word and wondered how it could possibly impact our lives. It's one thing to simply read the Bible. It's something different altogether to understand it. Far too often we read these stories about people in an ancient land, and we're left feeling flat. "What's this got to do with me?" We know in our hearts that what we're reading is true, right, and good, but we can't see any real way to apply it.

That's where *LIQUID* comes in.

LIQUID presents true-to-life stories of characters with real problems. Because what's the point in putting together a study of God's Word that doesn't deal with any of the issues we actually face? Along with each chapter in this book is a film, filled with characters who live in our world—the real world. Yet their problems and struggles mirror the same struggles found in stories in the Bible.

Jesus is the master storyteller. He helped people understand, made them contemplate, made them consider. He wasn't afraid to cut a story a couple of ways, as if he was saying, "Let me say it another way, a different way, so you can understand." He often gave answers by asking questions in return, so people would investigate, think, learn. It's how he did it, so it's why we do it. We translate ancient stories into the language of today's culture, and we ask relevant questions to help you discover the truth for yourself.

Whether you're with a small group, or simply by yourself, all we ask is that you take a deep breath, pop in the DVD, and then read through these pages and think carefully about the questions and the Scriptures. These are not questions from the SAT—they don't have definitive answers. They are designed for you to reflect upon based on your perspective. Everyone's discoveries will be different. But that's what's great about God's truth—it's one truth, but it's formed differently around each person.

It's simply about taking in, reflecting, and coming up with something useful for your life. Now at last we have an immediate, portable, relevant way to experience God's Word. A revolutionary new way to study the Bible.

LIQUID. God's Word flowing through your life.

▬ THE TEN: 6–10

When you think of the Ten Commandments, ancient tablets etched in stone, it's easy to disregard them as irrelevant and antiquated. Don't lie, don't steal, don't murder—they're all good ideas, of course, but do we really need a 3,500-year-old set of laws to guide us in this modern world?

In *The Ten: 6–10* we are once again introduced to the lives of men and women who forget God's fundamental truths and choose to live by their own set of rules. The consequences of ignoring God's laws can be devastating, but we will discover that God's love and redemption can be found even in the direst of circumstances.

CHAPTER 1: THE KILLER WITHIN

You must not murder (Exodus 20:13).

What's worse: a guilty person being set free or an innocent person being put away? This is a tough question. On one hand I have read stories of people who were guilty, but because of either a technicality or a lack of evidence they weren't convicted. Seeing this injustice made me angry for the victims and sad for their families. On the other hand I read a story about an innocent person who was imprisoned for twenty years before it came to light that he really didn't do it. Thinking about it gave me a pit in my stomach and shook my faith in our legal system. Both angles are gut-wrenching. But which is worse? Is that even possible to decide?

Which do you think is worse and why?

Play video episode now.

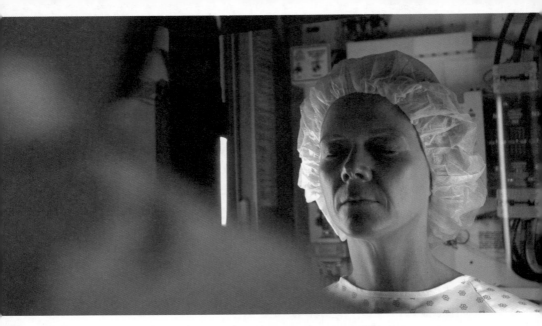

When I first saw the envelope, I was intrigued. What was inside? I was pretty sure it was something incriminating, something that he was willing to freeze a woman over. You might say I was dying to know what was inside. I had a feeling they were pictures, just not sure of what. As haunted as I was because I didn't know what was in the envelope, the good doctor was even more haunted because he did know the contents. Sure, the unknown contents were killing me, but not as much as they were killing him.

What are the murders, and how do they affect the characters in the story?

How does the original murder come back to haunt the doctor?

MATTHEW 5:21–22

²¹ "You have heard that our ancestors were told, 'You must not murder. If you commit murder, you are subject to judgment.' ²² But I say, if you are even angry with someone, you are subject to judgment! If you call someone an idiot, you are in danger of being brought before the court. And if you curse someone, you are in danger of the fires of hell."

1 JOHN 3:11–24

¹¹ This is the message you have heard from the beginning: We should love one another. ¹² We must not be like Cain, who belonged to the evil one and killed his brother. And why did he kill him? Because Cain had been doing what was evil, and his brother had been doing what was righteous. ¹³ So don't be surprised, dear brothers and sisters, if the world hates you.

¹⁴ If we love our Christian brothers and sisters, it proves that we have passed from death to life. But a person who has no love is still dead. ¹⁵ Anyone who hates another brother or sister is really a murderer at heart. And you know that murderers don't have eternal life within them.

¹⁶ We know what real love is because Jesus gave up his life for us. So we also ought to give up our lives for our brothers and sisters. ¹⁷ If someone has enough money to live well and sees a brother or sister in need but shows no compassion—how can God's love be in that person?

¹⁸ Dear children, let's not merely say that we love each other; let us show the truth by our actions. ¹⁹ Our actions will show that we belong to the truth, so we will be confident

when we stand before God. [20] Even if we feel guilty, God is greater than our feelings, and he knows everything.

[21] Dear friends, if we don't feel guilty, we can come to God with bold confidence. [22] And we will receive from him whatever we ask because we obey him and do the things that please him.

[23] And this is his commandment: We must believe in the name of his Son, Jesus Christ, and love one another, just as he commanded us. [24] Those who obey God's commandments remain in fellowship with him, and he with them. And we know he lives in us because the Spirit he gave us lives in us.

CULTURAL AND HISTORICAL THOUGHTS

Cain was the firstborn child of Adam and Eve. Eve later gave birth to Abel. Cain grew up and became a farmer, while Abel became a shepherd. Both Cain and Abel understood that the Lord requested the first and best of what they had to offer, but when it came time to present the sacrifice to the Lord, only Abel gave God his best. Abel offered his gifts with a heart of faith, while Cain offered his out of obligation.

God accepted Abel and his gift of sacrifice but rejected Cain and his gift. This angered Cain, and jealousy and bitterness burned in his heart. God presented Cain with a solution, but Cain chose to harbor his anger and let it consume him. His hatred toward his brother escalated and led him to coax Abel into the fields and kill him. This is the first premeditated murder in the Bible, and the ramifications for this sin were eternal.

Have you ever had your opinion of something turned upside down? When I was a kid, I hated cheesecake, but when I tried it again as an adult, it became the best thing I ever tasted. Or take my opinion of Nascar. I used to think it was a pointless sport, if it was even a sport at all. Then I had the opportunity to ride in a real race car and found out it was exciting and actually worthy of being called a sport. What about the definition of *murder*? It seems pretty black-and-white—you either kill someone or you don't. Then you read these passages, and what do Jesus and John do? They turn it upside down.

How do Jesus and John elaborate on the original commandment of "You must not murder"?

I have probably seen the footage of John F. Kennedy's assassination over a hundred times. I have heard the description over and over of how the bullet struck him: "back and to the left, back and to the left." It must have been frightening to see the president get murdered right in front of you. Right now I am sitting next to a guy in a coffee shop who is "murdering" our current president. That's right, murdering. He is spewing so much hatred that if words were bullets, the president would be dead. It may not be quite as frightening as the Kennedy assassination, but pretty close.

What are ways people "murder" each other today? What are the results?

Our neighbor down the street continuously drives way too fast past our house. And not only does she drive too fast, but she doesn't pay attention. I have four young kids who play outside all the time, and if anything ever happened to one of them, I would die. I have tried to tell her a few times to please slow down, but she doesn't seem to listen or care. One day after I witnessed a particularly fast incident, I stomped down to her house in a fury and asked her if it was going to take one of my kids getting run over for her to stop. I was pretty passionate. Well, last week I saw the same woman drive into our church parking lot on her way to a service. I guess my righteous anger wasn't so righteous after all.

Who are you "murdering" today? How does it affect the way you feel when you consider that you are breaking the commandment "You must not murder"?

What can you change to stop "murdering" others, and what will that look like in your life and theirs?

What would it look like to not just stop "murdering" (hating) them, but actually love them?

When I used to read through the Ten Commandments, I would check off the ones that I had committed. "You must not murder" was always my safety commandment, the one I could go back to when I needed to feel good about myself. After all, I've never killed anyone, never pulled out a gun or fired a bullet. And quite frankly, I could never in a thousand years imagine myself ever doing it. I thought as commandments went, I was safe with this one. Then a game changer: we're not only supposed to avoid killing people; we're not only supposed to avoid hating people; we are supposed to love people. I'm now realizing that when it comes to safety commandments, I seem to be running out.

EXTRA QUESTIONS

Why is it sometimes easier to hate than to love?

What are the benefits of loving instead of hating?

Are there any benefits to hating? If so, what are they?

Why is it difficult to love someone whom you have strong negative feelings toward?

What does it show to other people when you actually love someone, even after you have been wronged?

CHAPTER 2: CRAVE

*You must not commit adultery
(Exodus 20:14).*

I just got home. I've been away from my family on business for pretty much the last five weeks. I checked my calendar to see what my upcoming week was looking like, and then I remembered: I am scheduled to play golf with my buddies the next day. Wow, what a dilemma. It's my first day back with my family and I am supposed to go out and play golf. My eyes dart back and forth from my calendar to the "to do" list my wife has already handed me. What is a guy to do? Well, I do what any smart husband would do: I call my friends and say, "I'm gonna have to take a rain check." All through the day as I'm painting the coffee table, I am getting constant updates on their great round of golf. I could have gone, but honestly I'm glad I didn't. Well, maybe not glad, but at least I'm lucky I didn't.

Tell about a time you ran from something you could have done that might have hurt you (emotionally, physically, relationally, financially)—and were glad you did.

Play video episode now.

Things in my life I have had to clean up: a spill in the kitchen, a bucket of paint on the carpet, a pile of clothes in my kid's room. But the thought of cleaning up an affair like Alice had to—that's a whole new level of messiness. How do you make it right? Where do you start? Just thinking about speaking to the wife whose family you ruined gives me chills. I guess, though it is a start, it's the least that she could do. As I learn with every new spill, making the mess is quick and easy. Now cleaning it up, that's what takes time.

What are the effects that adultery has on all of the parties?

What healing might take place after Alice owns up to the wife regarding the affair?

MATTHEW 5:27–28 NIV

27 "You have heard that it was said, 'Do not commit adultery.' 28 But I tell you that anyone who looks at a woman lustfully has already committed adultery with her in his heart."

GENESIS 39 NIV

1 Now Joseph had been taken down to Egypt. Potiphar, an Egyptian who was one of Pharaoh's officials, the captain of the guard, bought him from the Ishmaelites who had taken him there.

2 The LORD was with Joseph and he prospered, and he lived in the house of his Egyptian master. 3 When his master saw that the LORD was with him and that the LORD gave him success in everything he did, 4 Joseph found favor in his eyes and became his attendant. Potiphar put him in charge of his household, and he entrusted to his care everything he owned. 5 From the time he put him in charge of his household and of all that he owned, the LORD blessed the household of the Egyptian because of Joseph. The blessing of the LORD was on everything Potiphar had, both in the house and in the field. 6 So he left in Joseph's care everything he had; with Joseph in charge, he did not concern himself with anything except the food he ate.

Now Joseph was well-built and handsome, 7 and after a while his master's wife took notice of Joseph and said, "Come to bed with me!"

[8] But he refused. "With me in charge," he told her, "my master does not concern himself with anything in the house; everything he owns he has entrusted to my care. [9] No one is greater in this house than I am. My master has withheld nothing from me except you, because you are his wife. How then could I do such a wicked thing and sin against God?" [10] And though she spoke to Joseph day after day, he refused to go to bed with her or even be with her.

[11] One day he went into the house to attend to his duties, and none of the household servants was inside. [12] She caught him by his cloak and said, "Come to bed with me!" But he left his cloak in her hand and ran out of the house.

[13] When she saw that he had left his cloak in her hand and had run out of the house, [14] she called her household servants. "Look," she said to them, "this Hebrew has been brought to us to make sport of us! He came in here to sleep with me, but I screamed. [15] When he heard me scream for help, he left his cloak beside me and ran out of the house."

[16] She kept his cloak beside her until his master came home. [17] Then she told him this story: "That Hebrew slave you brought us came to me to make sport of me. [18] But as soon as I screamed for help, he left his cloak beside me and ran out of the house."

¹⁹ When his master heard the story his wife told him, saying, "This is how your slave treated me," he burned with anger. ²⁰ Joseph's master took him and put him in prison, the place where the king's prisoners were confined.

But while Joseph was there in the prison, ²¹ the Lord was with him; he showed him kindness and granted him favor in the eyes of the prison warden. ²² So the warden put Joseph in charge of all those held in the prison, and he was made responsible for all that was done there. ²³ The warden paid no attention to anything under Joseph's care, because the Lord was with Joseph and gave him success in whatever he did.

CULTURAL AND HISTORICAL THOUGHTS

Joseph was one of twelve sons of Jacob, but he was the eldest son with Rachel, Jacob's true love. Rachel died during the birth of their second son, Benjamin. Joseph enjoyed favored status with his father for all of his life, causing much jealousy amidst his brothers. This jealousy led the brothers to conspire to kill Joseph when they were traveling away from their father. Instead they sold him as a slave to some Ishmaelites, who were Midianite traders, passing by. The traders paid Joseph's brothers twenty pieces of silver and then took him to Egypt, where he was eventually sold again to Potiphar. The remaining brothers then told Jacob a wild beast had killed Joseph, his favorite son, and Jacob went into mourning.

After the event with Potiphar's wife, Joseph spent time in jail alongside Pharaoh's chief cup-bearer and baker. While in jail he interpreted dreams for them that proved true. Two years later Pharaoh had a dream that no one was able to interpret. The cup-bearer remembered Joseph, and Pharaoh sent for him. Joseph explained that Pharaoh's dream indicated that Egypt would undergo seven years of abundance followed by seven years of famine. Pharaoh knew Joseph was filled with the Spirit of God and made him second-in-command.

During the seven years of abundance, Joseph amassed huge harvests for Pharaoh, and the storehouses were filled with plenty of supplies to last throughout the coming seven years of famine. But not everyone was prepared, and many people came to Joseph to purchase food, including his own brothers. Thirteen years had passed, and Joseph had aged to the point that his brothers did not recognize him. But Joseph recognized them. He could have waged revenge against his brothers, and most would have considered it warranted. But instead he offered them forgiveness and gave them the best land and plenty of food as symbols of their reconciliation.

It looks like a story straight from *Desperate Housewives*—the passionate woman going after the hired help. Of course on television, there is not much drama unless the guy gives in and the tension unfolds. But I have to be honest: this is an incredible story, and what do you know, it is a story about a guy who does the right thing. Who says nice guys always finish last? Of course, Joseph does the right thing and ends up in jail. But trust me, the story works out well in the end. Well, maybe not for the "desperate housewife," but ultimately for Joseph.

From the Matthew passage, what do you learn about adultery?

From the Genesis passage, what do you learn about Potiphar's wife and Joseph? What helped Joseph to not give in, but flee instead?

Every now and then I find myself watching ESPN2. Nowadays there always seems to be a poker tournament on. The players oftentimes seem more intriguing than the game itself. There is always such a sense of drama, with the men and women hiding behind their sunglasses and hats, and taking forever to play their cards, which only makes the game drag incredibly long. Last week I was ready to change channels, but then they did something intriguing—they turned it into a million-dollar pot. With one simple motion, they upped the ante and things got a lot more interesting. It's what Jesus did in the Sermon on the Mount. With a few simple words, he raised the stakes and made things a lot more interesting.

With the expanded definition of the commandment in mind, how do you see people committing "adultery" today? What are the results?

What helps people to not give in to the temptation, but flee from it instead?

As a pastor I live by some safeguards that my church expects from its employees, and I have to say, I'm glad they have them. For example, I am not allowed to have a one-on-one meal with another woman. I am not allowed to drive in the car alone with a woman who is not my wife. My friend has a rule where he will never text-message another woman. Some people call these things going a little overboard, but I just like to think that I am guarding one of my most precious possessions—my marriage.

> What are some practical steps you can take to safeguard your marriage or relationship and flee when tempted?

When am I most susceptible? I would like to think I am never susceptible to the temptation of adultery. I have always lived by the saying "Avoid the catastrophe," and in my mind adultery is a catastrophe. Now, when am I susceptible to lust? That's a different story. I think as a guy that temptation is always before me. But I have to say, when I am disconnected from my wife, I am even more on guard. Why is that? Well, that would take a few pages, so let's just leave it at that. I know when to be on guard.

EXTRA QUESTIONS

When is it easier to flee and when is it more difficult?

What are times in your life you are more susceptible to the temptation of lust?

What are some of the things you do to combat the temptation of lust?

What are some of the ramifications of adultery in the lives of people?

When was a time in your life you acted in the same manner as Joseph?

Why is lust such a difficult issue for men?

Why is lust a difficult issue for women?

CHAPTER 3: TAKE THAT

You must not steal (Exodus 20:15).

Don't call my parents, don't call my parents. It was all I could think about when my buddies and I were nabbed at the local supermarket for stealing a candy bar. The manager had been staking us out, watching us grab candy bars from his store for three days in a row. As I was listening to him read us the riot act, I was kicking myself internally, thinking, *Never return to the scene of the crime, stupid!*, like I was some cagey cat burglar. He put quite a scare in us, although thankfully it just turned out to be a slap on the wrist and a stern "never come back here again."

Did you ever steal something growing up? Did you get caught?

Play video episode now.

In baseball you can steal bases, an opportunity to get ahead and further your position. It's a ninety-foot sprint, usually ending with a slide that leaves the runner in a pile of dust and dirt. But what about actually stealing, taking a possession that doesn't belong to you? Usually that "I want it" feeling is motivated by greed, or revenge, or just flat-out desperation. It is seeing an opportunity to get something or have something that you can't quite get on your own and just grabbing it. The interesting thing is, when you steal a base in baseball you get dirty, but when you steal something in life, you feel dirty.

What are all of the things that are stolen? What are the motivations that the characters have to justify stealing?

²⁷ As the boys grew up, Esau became a skillful hunter. He was an outdoorsman, but Jacob had a quiet temperament, preferring to stay at home. ²⁸ Isaac loved Esau because he enjoyed eating the wild game Esau brought home, but Rebekah loved Jacob.

²⁹ One day when Jacob was cooking some stew, Esau arrived home from the wilderness exhausted and hungry. ³⁰ Esau said to Jacob, "I'm starved! Give me some of that red stew!" (This is how Esau got his other name, Edom, which means "red.")

³¹ "All right," Jacob replied, "but trade me your rights as the firstborn son."

³² "Look, I'm dying of starvation!" said Esau. "What good is my birthright to me now?"

³³ But Jacob said, "First you must swear that your birthright is mine." So Esau swore an oath, thereby selling all his rights as the firstborn to his brother, Jacob.

³⁴ Then Jacob gave Esau some bread and lentil stew. Esau ate the meal, then got up and left. He showed contempt for his rights as the firstborn.

[1] One day when Isaac was old and turning blind, he called for Esau, his older son, and said, "My son."

"Yes, Father?" Esau replied.

[2] "I am an old man now," Isaac said, "and I don't know when I may die. [3] Take your bow and a quiver full of arrows, and go out into the open country to hunt some wild game for me. [4] Prepare my favorite dish, and bring it here for me to eat. Then I will pronounce the blessing that belongs to you, my firstborn son, before I die."

[5] But Rebekah overheard what Isaac had said to his son Esau. So when Esau left to hunt for the wild game, [6] she said to her son Jacob, "Listen. I overheard your father say to Esau, [7] 'Bring me some wild game and prepare me a delicious meal. Then I will bless you in the LORD's presence before I die.' [8] Now, my son, listen to me. Do exactly as I tell you. [9] Go out to the flocks, and bring me two fine young goats. I'll use them to prepare your father's favorite dish. [10] Then take the food to your father so he can eat it and bless you before he dies."

[11] "But look," Jacob replied to Rebekah, "my brother, Esau, is a hairy man, and my skin is smooth. [12] What if my father touches me? He'll see that I'm trying to trick him, and then he'll curse me instead of blessing me."

[13] But his mother replied, "Then let the curse fall on me, my son! Just do what I tell you. Go out and get the goats for me!"

¹⁴ So Jacob went out and got the young goats for his mother. Rebekah took them and prepared a delicious meal, just the way Isaac liked it. ¹⁵ Then she took Esau's favorite clothes, which were there in the house, and gave them to her younger son, Jacob. ¹⁶ She covered his arms and the smooth part of his neck with the skin of the young goats. ¹⁷ Then she gave Jacob the delicious meal, including freshly baked bread.

¹⁸ So Jacob took the food to his father. "My father?" he said.

"Yes, my son," Isaac answered. "Who are you—Esau or Jacob?"

¹⁹ Jacob replied, "It's Esau, your firstborn son. I've done as you told me. Here is the wild game. Now sit up and eat it so you can give me your blessing."

²⁰ Isaac asked, "How did you find it so quickly, my son?"

"The LORD your God put it in my path!" Jacob replied.

²¹ Then Isaac said to Jacob, "Come closer so I can touch you and make sure that you really are Esau." ²² So Jacob went closer to his father, and Isaac touched him. "The voice is Jacob's, but the hands are Esau's," Isaac said. ²³ But he did not recognize Jacob, because Jacob's hands felt hairy just like Esau's. So Isaac prepared to bless Jacob. ²⁴ "But are you really my son Esau?" he asked.

"Yes, I am," Jacob replied.

²⁵ Then Isaac said, "Now, my son, bring me the wild game. Let me eat it, and then I will give you my blessing." So Jacob took the food to his father, and Isaac ate it. He also drank the wine that Jacob served him. Then Isaac said to Jacob, ²⁶ "Please come a little closer and kiss me, my son."

27 So Jacob went over and kissed him. And when Isaac caught the smell of his clothes, he was finally convinced, and he blessed his son. He said, "Ah! The smell of my son is like the smell of the outdoors, which the LORD has blessed!

28 "From the dew of heaven and the richness of the earth,
may God always give you abundant harvests of grain and bountiful new wine.

29 May many nations become your servants, and may they bow down to you.
May you be the master over your brothers, and may your mother's sons bow down to you.
All who curse you will be cursed, and all who bless you will be blessed."

30 As soon as Isaac had finished blessing Jacob, and almost before Jacob had left his father, Esau returned from his hunt. 31 Esau prepared a delicious meal and brought it to his father. Then he said, "Sit up, my father, and eat my wild game so you can give me your blessing."

32 But Isaac asked him, "Who are you?"
Esau replied, "It's your son, your firstborn son, Esau."

33 Isaac began to tremble uncontrollably and said, "Then who just served me wild game? I have already eaten it, and I blessed him just before you came. And yes, that blessing must stand!"

[34] When Esau heard his father's words, he let out a loud and bitter cry. "Oh my father, what about me? Bless me, too!" he begged.

[35] But Isaac said, "Your brother was here, and he tricked me. He has taken away your blessing."

[36] Esau exclaimed, "No wonder his name is Jacob, for now he has cheated me twice. First he took my rights as the firstborn, and now he has stolen my blessing. Oh, haven't you saved even one blessing for me?"

[37] Isaac said to Esau, "I have made Jacob your master and have declared that all his brothers will be his servants. I have guaranteed him an abundance of grain and wine—what is left for me to give you, my son?"

[38] Esau pleaded, "But do you have only one blessing? Oh my father, bless me, too!" Then Esau broke down and wept.

[39] Finally, his father, Isaac, said to him,

"You will live away from the richness of the earth,

and away from the dew of the heaven above.

[40] You will live by your sword,

and you will serve your brother.

But when you decide to break free,

you will shake his yoke from your neck."

CULTURAL AND HISTORICAL THOUGHTS

Birthright and blessings were the most important inheritance of firstborn males. In ancient Asiatic culture, the firstborn son was anointed with the assignment of special privileges and responsibilities. He was second to his father and had authority over his younger siblings. Upon his father's death, he was entitled to the birthright, which was a double portion of the estate and leadership of the family. If there were four sons in the family, the estate would be divided by five, with two-fifths being given to the oldest and one-fifth to each of the other sons. As new head and spiritual leader of the home, the firstborn cared for his mother until her death, and provided for his unmarried sisters until their marriage.

Esau, in a moment of weakness and hunger, sold his birthright to his younger brother, Jacob. His hunger caused him to forfeit his birthright for some lentil stew. Jacob willingly accepted his brother's birthright, knowing well that it wasn't an even trade.

The story of Jacob stealing the blessing from Esau came years after the birthright had been forfeited, and of course fulfilled the words that God had spoken while Rebekah was still pregnant with the brothers. Jacob and Esau went on to lead separate lives in separate parts of the world, and although Jacob had received both the birthright and blessing, in the end it was Jacob who had to flee with nothing but his staff and the shirt on his back. Twenty-one years later, the two brothers, each blessed with wealth, were brought back together for an honest reconciliation, which allowed them to carry out important tasks, including the burial of their father, Isaac.

You've heard the saying "Never go shopping when you are hungry." Why is that? Because when you are hungry you overbuy and make bad decisions. No one understands that better than Esau. A birthright was a lot to give up, especially for only a meal. Both of the brothers' decision making was incredibly questionable, but there is a difference. One son was just hasty, while the other was downright deceptive. I have to imagine that Jacob not only stole the blessing from Esau but also ripped the heart out of Isaac.

What are the reasons Jacob stole the birthright and blessing?

What all was involved in Jacob and Rebekah stealing Esau's birthright and blessing?

What were the results?

Last week I was at the coffee shop, purchasing a large coffee and a muffin. I went up to pay and their credit card machine was down. They were only accepting cash. Well, that was a problem because I don't normally carry cash on me. I told the cashier and she was very understanding, telling me I could just bring it by later. When I went by that afternoon, I was in a big hurry, and the line was so long I couldn't wait. It's been a week and I still haven't gone back. To be honest, I forgot about it until I started writing this. In a subtle way, I am stealing. I'll be heading over this week. I feel more than just compelled to; I feel commanded.

What are ways, even the most subtle, that people "steal" today? What are the results (both good and bad)?

I came home and my wife was holding up a shopping bag, clearly excited about her purchases. She had a big smile on her face when she told me that the purchases were actually for me. She began to lay out four new shirts, all of which she says she loves, and all of which she got a great deal on. I wish I had been at least half as excited about the shirts as she was. I did what I typically do. I said, "They're OK." As I watched the excitement drain from her face, I realized that Jeff the Joy Stealer has struck again. I don't mean to do it, but when people meet me with enthusiasm I can be a downer and unknowingly respond in the wrong way. I guess you could say at times I'm not just a joy stealer, but I am a master thief.

In what areas of your life are you "stealing," and from whom are you "stealing"?

How does the fact that you are breaking the commandment "You must not steal" affect how you feel about it?

What lesson will you take away from this week's study, and how will it change your actions?

When I got out to the curb, I could see the glass on the ground and I knew exactly what had happened. My car had been broken into. Papers were strewn about in my car, and there was a hole where my radio used to be. I actually had a smile on my face because that thief stole the biggest piece-of-junk car radio you could imagine, complete with a broken cassette deck and everything. I almost felt as though I came out ahead in that aspect, because I had been meaning to replace it anyway. The hard part was dealing with that little part inside me that felt violated, ticked off that someone had invaded my personal space. Two days later, I wanted to hit golf balls so I went to the garage and my heart dropped—my golf clubs had been in my car that day and I only now remembered them. Turns out a lot was stolen after all.

EXTRA QUESTIONS

How do you steal things, other than possessions, from people?

Make a list of things that could be considered stealing that we don't really think anything about.

Have you ever had anything stolen from you? How did it make you feel?

What are some of the reasons people steal?

What does stealing do to the person who was stolen from? How might it affect the person who stole?

CHAPTER 4: SHADES OF GREY

You must not testify falsely against your neighbor (Exodus 20:16).

I love the game Two Truths and a Lie. I remember playing as a kid growing up. Let's play a quick round: My first time scuba diving I came face-to-face with the biggest shark I have ever seen; I was the first-round pick of the New York Yankees in 1984; I have ridden shotgun in an F-16 fighter jet. OK, your turn to tell me which one is the lie. Here's a hint: I hate heights, even ladders.

Play a round of Two Truths and a Lie and have people try to guess the lie.

Play video episode now.

What do you do as a kid if you are questioned about the truth? You "prove" that you're telling the truth by adding in lines like "cross my heart, hope to die." What do you do if you are a kid and you want to lie? You secretly hide your hands, so you don't let people see that you are crossing your fingers. As an adult, those things don't work; "cross my heart, hope to die" is just a little juvenile. Thinking that you can just cross your fingers and then lie is something adults don't do. What else don't adults do? Put their hand on the Bible, promise to tell the truth, and then lie. You see, that's not just juvenile; that is against the law. You can go to jail for that, and believe me, I'm not crossing my fingers when I say that.

How do the characters lie?

What is the stance they have for justifying their lies?

How did their lies come back to haunt them?

[32] All the believers were united in heart and mind. And they felt that what they owned was not their own, so they shared everything they had. [33] The apostles testified powerfully to the resurrection of the Lord Jesus, and God's great blessing was upon them all. [34] There were no needy people among them, because those who owned land or houses would sell them [35] and bring the money to the apostles to give to those in need.

[36] For instance, there was Joseph, the one the apostles nicknamed Barnabas (which means "Son of Encouragement"). He was from the tribe of Levi and came from the island of Cyprus. [37] He sold a field he owned and brought the money to the apostles.

[5:1] But there was a certain man named Ananias who, with his wife, Sapphira, sold some property. [2] He brought part of the money to the apostles, claiming it was the full amount. With his wife's consent, he kept the rest.

[3] Then Peter said, "Ananias, why have you let Satan fill your heart? You lied to the Holy Spirit, and you kept some of the money for yourself. [4] The property was yours to sell or not sell, as you wished. And after selling it, the money was also yours to give away. How could you do a thing like this? You weren't lying to us but to God!"

[5] As soon as Ananias heard these words, he fell to the floor and died. Everyone who heard about it was terrified. [6] Then some young men got up, wrapped him in a sheet, and took him out and buried him.

[7] About three hours later his wife came in, not knowing what had happened.

[8] Peter asked her, "Was this the price you and your husband received for your land?"

"Yes," she replied, "that was the price."

⁹ And Peter said, "How could the two of you even think of conspiring to test the Spirit of the Lord like this? The young men who buried your husband are just outside the door, and they will carry you out, too."

¹⁰ Instantly, she fell to the floor and died. When the young men came in and saw that she was dead, they carried her out and buried her beside her husband. ¹¹ Great fear gripped the entire church and everyone else who heard what had happened.

CULTURAL AND HISTORICAL THOUGHTS

The early Christians believed that nothing they had acquired was owned by them and decided to share everything they had. Those who owned property sold it and gave the money to the apostles to make sure the needy were taken care of. This philosophy was akin to a Jewish law that made caring for the poor a requirement of the more fortunate. However, since the new believers in Jesus Christ were considered heretics, they were not eligible to participate in the Jewish custom. So it was with a voluntary outpouring of love in which the wealthier believers continued the practice within the new church. By holding back the money from the property they sold, Ananias and Sapphira were blatantly desregarding these practices.

This story always throws me for a loop. It is a wake-up call for me that God is really serious about some things. A part of me always wrote off stories like this because they were normally found in the Old Testament, and God in the Old Testament was much harder on people than God in the New Testament, right? I mean, after Jesus came on the scene, God seemed to mellow out and become more easygoing. But here it is—a story in the New Testament where two people drop dead for lying. This really changes my thinking. Right is right and wrong is wrong, and God cares about sin regardless of where or when it happens. Now if I was to drop dead every time I told a lie or withheld from God, I would be a dead man walking. Nevertheless, God is very serious about sin.

What do you learn about those who keep their word and those who deceive?

I was in a Bible study with some friends fifteen years ago, and I remember that one of the topics we discussed was about lying and telling the truth. One of my friends shared about how he used to run his personal letters through the company's stamp machine; he would just claim that they were business related. Even though it was just ten cents—no big deal, right?—he still realized he was lying. I remember thinking to myself, *That's silly that he even considers that lying.* To this day, however, when I take an outgoing letter to the receptionist and ask her to stamp and mail it for me, she always asks, "Personal or business?" There are times when I don't have any money on me and am tempted to say "business," but I just can't. I guess now my friend's dilemma doesn't seem as silly to me anymore.

What are ways (no matter how subtle) people deceive others today?

Why do people deceive others?

What happens when someone keeps their word? What are the results when they don't?

I grabbed my briefcase, patted all my kids on the head, and told them to have a great day at school. I then went over to my wife and kissed her good-bye and told her that I was off to work. And technically I was. What I didn't tell her was that I had gotten up early and stashed my golf clubs in the car; I was going to sneak off and play golf with friends after I spent about an hour at work. I don't know why I didn't just tell her. I guess I felt guilty because she was home with the kids and I would be off having fun. Technically I did go to work, but in reality I was stretching the truth. I've never told her that I played golf that day—well, until now. Looks like I have a little explaining and apologizing to do.

In what areas of your life do you find it easy to keep your word, and in what areas are you deceitful, even in the most subtle of ways?

When you consider that even little white lies are breaking the commandment, how does that affect what you'll say going forward?

I have heard it said that it takes years to create integrity but only a moment to lose it. I don't necessarily know if that is true, or even fair. But in my mind that is what lying does—it just clips a person's integrity a bit. Lying has a secretive element to it, and if you are caught lying about one element of your life, people start to wonder when else you have lied. Trustworthiness enhances a feeling of connectedness with other people. People draw close to those they trust, or those with whom they feel safe. If you want to be close to people, a great place to start is being trustworthy.

EXTRA QUESTIONS

What are some of the reasons people justify lying?

What is it like being around someone who is trustworthy?
What is it like being with someone who isn't?

If you tell even the most subtle of lies, how does it impact
your relationship with others? With God?

What is it that keeps you from lying?

CHAPTER 5: MINE!

You must not covet (Exodus 20:17).

Most of my friends have one. They flaunt it in front of me, and make me feel like I still live in the Dark Ages. When I need directions, they whip it out. When they want to share their favorite song, it comes in handy. When we are at some cool place and we need to snap a photo, no problem, they can take care of it. You guessed it, the dreaded iPhone. I don't hate it; I actually admire it. I am enamored by it, intrigued by it. I don't just want one; I am convinced I have to have one.

What is something you don't have that you would love to get?

Play video episode now.

Love or money? It's a tough choice . . . for some people. Aaron, a guy who has found the love of his life, just found something he loves even more. The girl is nice to have, but the job is something he has to have. Problem is, he has the girl; the job isn't in the bag yet. The position that he has to have, needs to have, is so compelling that he's even willing to give up the love of his life in order to get it. You might say he loves the girl, but covets the opportunity for the job of a lifetime.

What are the things that Aaron covets? What is he willing to give up in order to get what he wants? How does he come to grips and stop coveting?

¹ Now there was a man named Naboth, from Jezreel, who owned a vineyard in Jezreel beside the palace of King Ahab of Samaria. ² One day Ahab said to Naboth, "Since your vineyard is so convenient to my palace, I would like to buy it to use as a vegetable garden. I will give you a better vineyard in exchange, or if you prefer, I will pay you for it."

³ But Naboth replied, "The LORD forbid that I should give you the inheritance that was passed down by my ancestors."

⁴ So Ahab went home angry and sullen because of Naboth's answer. The king went to bed with his face to the wall and refused to eat!

⁵ "What's the matter?" his wife Jezebel asked him. "What's made you so upset that you're not eating?"

⁶ "I asked Naboth to sell me his vineyard or trade it, but he refused!" Ahab told her.

⁷ "Are you the king of Israel or not?" Jezebel demanded. "Get up and eat something, and don't worry about it. I'll get you Naboth's vineyard!"

⁸ So she wrote letters in Ahab's name, sealed them with his seal, and sent them to the elders and other leaders of the town where Naboth lived. ⁹ In her letters she commanded: "Call the citizens together for fasting and prayer, and give Naboth a place of honor. ¹⁰ And then seat two scoundrels across from him who will accuse him of cursing God and the king. Then take him out and stone him to death."

¹¹ So the elders and other town leaders followed the instructions Jezebel had written in the letters. ¹² They called for a fast and put Naboth at a prominent place before the

people. ¹³ Then the two scoundrels came and sat down across from him. And they accused Naboth before all the people, saying, "He cursed God and the king." So he was dragged outside the town and stoned to death. ¹⁴ The town leaders then sent word to Jezebel, "Naboth has been stoned to death."

¹⁵ When Jezebel heard the news, she said to Ahab, "You know the vineyard Naboth wouldn't sell you? Well, you can have it now! He's dead!" ¹⁶ So Ahab immediately went down to the vineyard of Naboth to claim it.

¹⁷ But the Lord said to Elijah, ¹⁸ "Go down to meet King Ahab of Israel, who rules in Samaria. He will be at Naboth's vineyard in Jezreel, claiming it for himself. ¹⁹ Give him this message: 'This is what the Lord says: Wasn't it enough that you killed Naboth? Must you rob him, too? Because you have done this, dogs will lick your blood at the very place where they licked the blood of Naboth!'"

²⁰ "So, my enemy, you have found me!" Ahab exclaimed to Elijah.

"Yes," Elijah answered, "I have come because you have sold yourself to what is evil in the Lord's sight. ²¹ So now the Lord says, 'I will bring disaster on you and consume you. I will destroy every one of your male descendants, slave and free alike, anywhere in Israel! ²² I am going to destroy your family as I did the family of Jeroboam son of Nebat and the family of Baasha son of Ahijah, for you have made me very angry and have led Israel into sin.'"

CULTURAL AND HISTORICAL THOUGHTS

Ahab was the seventh king of Israel's Northern Kingdom and has the unique and unfortunate reputation of angering God more than any of Israel's former kings. He married Jezebel, who was a Phoenician princess, and together they reigned for twenty years. This union provided both commercial and political benefits. However, Jezebel's father, the king of Sidon, worshiped Baal, not Yahweh, and Jezebel introduced this false god to Israel. Although Ahab appears to have been a worshiper of Yahweh, God of Israel, he most likely also worshiped other deities.

Jezebel held great power, managing not only her husband but 850 assorted pagan priests as well. She systematically tried to kill all of God's prophets in Israel and replace them with prophets of Baal and Asherah as part of the royal household. Even though Ahab consulted with the prophets of Yahweh, Jezebel's influence was much stronger and he did not interfere when she executed the prophets. The Baal prophets were proved false by one of God's prophets, Elijah, which angered Jezebel to the point of threatening to kill him. Jezebel contributed to the downfall of the Northern Kingdom, which was idolatry.

The main palace was in the capital city at Samaria. Among other things, it contained an opulent palace and a temple to Baal and Asherah. A second royal house was built near Jezreel. It was a villa, overlooking rolling hills and lush vineyards. Near the villa at Jezreel was the vineyard of Naboth. Ahab needed to amalgamate this land into the land owned by the royal villa in order to grow crops to feed the administrative and military staff living there. He made a fair offer to Naboth, but Naboth did not wish to sell. Jezebel believed kings and queens had the right to own anything they wanted. It was this belief that led her to manipulate the ruthless death of Naboth to obtain his vineyard for Ahab.

She continued her evil influence after Ahab was killed in battle and their son Joram ruled Israel. Jehu, anointed by Elisha to be the king to replace Joram, assassinated Joram and sought to kill Jezebel as well. She tried to manipulate Jehu and win him over, but her servants obeyed Jehu and threw her from the window to the street, where horses trampled her to death.

Jezebel's name became associated with wickedness and evil in the Bible to the point that those who reject God are known as "Jezebel."

My wife has a tendency to get a little more riled up than I do, be a little feistier. If she gets upset about something, I usually tell her, "Honey, I'll handle it." But heck, she is nothing like Ahab's wife. Talk about the wrath of a woman. The epitome of coveting—wanting something so badly that you are willing to kill for it. I have heard the term "to die for"; but to kill for, now that is a whole different story.

What are the ways Ahab and Jezebel coveted, and what were the results?

Who doesn't have desires? I mean, if you don't desire, you're dead. One of my favorite books of all time is *The Journey of Desire* by John Eldredge. It changed my life. I had shut down the desires of my life, thinking to myself I would never obtain anything, so why go for it? This book taught me that desiring is actually a good thing, that we should be the kind of people who go after things. All of us are created with desires in our lives—good, healthy, productive desires. To desire is to live.

What is the difference between desire and coveting? What makes people move from having a healthy desire to coveting?

We just finished remodeling our house. We actually lived in the house while we remodeled it, but that's another story. As I got more into the process, it was strange what happened to me. The more we did, the more I wanted to do. I started to play the game of, "Well, if we're doing this, why don't we just do it bigger and better?" Once we started knocking things down and retiling, I upped the ante from things I just wanted to do to things I had to do. I've always wanted to have a nice house, a really nice house, and this was finally my chance. When it comes to the difference between desiring and coveting, I'm not sure where I fell in this instance, but just the fact that I have to think about it is not a good sign.

Where in your life do you struggle with keeping your desires in check?

If you have coveted in the past (or struggle with it now), how does it affect your life?

What are some practical steps you can take to keep from coveting?

I want to be a great husband. I want my kids to admire me. I want to be an incredible father for them. I want to be a provider for my family. I want to be able to do things physically that I've always been able to do. I want to grow old gracefully. I want to be used by God and try to help people find God. I want to travel the world. I want to help my kids be the best they can be. And I can go on and on and on. I'm no different than you. Is it possible to have too many desires? I don't think so. I say it's better to have too many than not enough.

EXTRA QUESTIONS

Where do you have healthy desire for things in your life?

How have you seen coveting change people's lives?

What are things in this world that people have a tendency to covet?

How have you seen the things that people covet change over the years?

What keeps you from coveting?

What are some of the reasons that may increase your desire to covet?

▰ NOTE TO LEADERS

As leaders, we have tried to make this experience as easy for you as possible. Don't try to do too much during your time together as a group——just ask and listen, and direct when necessary.

The questions have a flow, a progression, and are designed to get people talking. If you help the group start talking early on, they will continue to talk. You will notice that the questions start out easy and casual, creating a theme. The theme continues throughout the session, flowing through casual topics, then into world affairs, and then they begin getting personal.

When the questions ask about the Bible, spend time there. Dig in and scour the passage. Keep looking. You and your group will discover that looking into the Bible can be fun and interesting. Maybe you already know that, but there will be people in your group who don't——people who are afraid of their Bibles, or who don't think they can really study them.

Remember, we are seeking life change. This will happen by taking God's Word and applying it to your life, and to the lives of the people you are with. That's the goal for each person in the group. Fight for it.

■ TIPS

So, are you a little nervous? Guess what—I get scared too. I always have a little apprehension when it comes to leading a group. It's what keeps me on my toes! Here are some things to keep in mind as you're preparing.

Think about your group. How does this week's topic relate to your group? Is this going to be an easy session? Is this going to be a challenge? The more at ease you are with the topic, the better the experience will be for your group.

Go over the leader's material early, and try to get to know the questions. Sometimes there are multiple questions provided at the end of the chapters. These are extra questions that can be used as supplemental questions at any point throughout the discussion. Look over these extra questions and see if any of them jump out at you. Don't feel that you have to address each question, but they are there if you need them. My worst nightmare is to be leading a group, and, with thirty minutes still left on the clock, we run out of questions and there's nothing left to talk about . . . so we sit there and stare at one another in painful silence.

Just remember to keep moving through all the questions. The most important goal of this study is to get personal and see how to apply biblical truths to your own life. When you're talking about how a passage plays out in the world today, a common mistake is to not take it deep enough . . . not to push the envelope and move it from what "they" should do to what "I" should do. As a leader, you will struggle with how much to push, how deep to dig. Sometimes it will be just right, sometimes you will push too hard, or sometimes not hard enough. Though it can be nerve-racking, it's the essence of being a leader.

Here are a few more tips:

- Get them talking, laughing, and having fun.
- Don't squelch emotion. Though it may tend to make you uncomfortable, to the point where you'll want to step in and rescue the moment, remember that leaders shouldn't always interfere.
- Jump in when needed. If the question is tough, make sure to model the answer. Try to be open about your own life. Often, the group will only go as deep as you are willing to go.
- When you look in the Bible for answers, don't quit too soon. Let people really search.
- Don't be afraid of silence.
- Lead the group—don't dominate it.

These are just a few things to think about before you begin.

▰▰ CHAPTER 1: THE KILLER WITHIN

▌ What do you think is worse—a guilty person being set free or an innocent person being put away? Why?

Leader note: This should cause a little bit of tension, but encourage participation by each group member. It is a conflicting question and could be pretty hard to choose a side. Have your group think of famous cases where they were convinced the guilty went free or where an innocent victim faced a life in prison for a crime he didn't commit. Several cases of people incarcerated for murder are being challenged with new DNA testing that proves they didn't commit the crime, yet they sit waiting for a new trial. So, which is worse?

Leader tip: Although this question will most likely cause a lot of discussion, don't get stuck here. Plan to allow about five minutes and then move on.

▌ How do Jesus and John elaborate on the original commandment of "You must not murder"?

Jesus
Being angry at someone is considered murder.
Calling someone an idiot or cursing them is considered murder.

John

We should love each other.

Don't be like Cain, who killed his brother.

He belonged to the evil one.

He had been doing what was evil.

Abel (the brother) was doing what was righteous.

If we love each other, we have passed from death to life.

A person who doesn't love is still dead.

If you hate someone, you are a murderer at heart.

Murderers don't have eternal life within them.

Real love is giving up your life for another.

Love is showing compassion and giving to those in need.

We should show it, not just say it.

If we love, we can be confident before God.

God knows what is behind our feelings—he knows everything.

We can come to God with bold confidence if we aren't guilty.

If we obey him and aren't guilty, we can boldly ask God and he will answer our prayers.

We are commanded to believe in Jesus and love one another.

If we obey, we remain in fellowship with God.

The Spirit lives in those who obey.

■ **What are ways people "murder" each other today? What are the results?**

Leader note: When you consider that murder includes being angry, harboring bitterness or hatred toward another person, or any derivative of anger, you can see that people "murder" each other all the time.

Commentary: A harsh word or any unloving activity results in a piece of a relationship dying, especially if it isn't addressed and repaired immediately. It seems our closest relationships are the ones we murder most often: A spouse reacts angrily to a comment, the silent treatment ensues, and the result is dying intimacy. Parents rage at their kids and say things they can't take back, and the relationship suffers. Children hold on to grudges against their siblings and parents, and the bitterness kills the family bond. Best friends become angry and allow the anger to take root and turn into resentment, and before you know it the friendship is lost completely.

> **Who are you "murdering" today? How does it affect the way you feel when you consider that you are breaking the commandment "You must not murder"?**

Leader note: It should really change the way you look at your anger when you consider it is breaking one of the Ten Commandments. It is easy to let our anger fly and hold on to hate when we believe it is merely an emotion, especially when we feel justified in our rage. But when we think about the fact that God had a top-ten list of things he couldn't tolerate and Jesus explained one of them as meaning we should not let anger remain in our lives, building to bitterness and hate, it changes things.

Leader tip: This can be a tough question for your group to answer—you are basically asking them to confess to breaking a commandment, something most people aren't eager to do! So model the answer by responding first. Talk about a relationship you have not tended to well, one where you feel you have responded in anger or let diminish because of resentment. How does it make you feel when you bear in mind you have broken a commandment?

> **What can you change to stop "murdering" others, and what will that look like in your life and theirs?**

Commentary: Some techniques you've heard since childhood may come to mind immediately: take a breath, count to ten before you speak, and consider the consequences of your anger; make amends as soon as you can; don't go to bed angry; resolve to apologize and ask for forgiveness when you let anger fly; commit to try to reconcile old relationships damaged by anger and resentment. The results of this type of restraint will be immediate. Those you love will most likely reciprocate with more loving actions. You will most likely be more intimate, more honest, believing that your relationships are safer.

> **What would it look like to not just stop "murdering" (hating) them, but actually love them?**

Leader tip: Have people take that extra step and come up with ideas of what it would look like to actually love people with whom they are struggling. Not be neutral, but actually love.

Extra questions: As always, use these questions to add to any conversation, or if you need further discussion. If you like these questions better, you can even substitute.

▬▬ CHAPTER 2: CRAVE

▌ **Tell about a time you ran from something you could have done that might have hurt you (emotionally, physically, relationally, financially)—and were glad you did.**

Leader note: We are trying to highlight the "fleeing" concept here. Lead your group to think about a time when they ran from something that was enticing—and available—to them instead of indulging in it. It might be a flirtatious relationship that could have gone further, or an investment that sounded too good to be true. Maybe someone in your group is a daredevil and wanted to try something completely death-defying and backed out because of the risks to health or family. Try to cover a bunch of different scenarios to increase the emotion from fleeing danger.

■ **From the Matthew passage, what do you learn about adultery?**

Commentary: Even looking at someone with lust in your heart is adultery.

▌ **From the Genesis passage, what do you learn about Potiphar's wife and Joseph? What helped Joseph to not give in, but flee instead?**

Leader tip: It may be helpful to look at Potiphar's wife first and discuss her actions, and then look at Joseph and how he responded to her and his motivation behind his actions.

Commentary (some of the observations your group should find):

Potiphar's Wife
- She was in a position of power since she was the boss's wife.
- Her husband was a powerful man.
- She took notice of Joseph because of his good looks and asked him to go to bed with her.
- She pursued him and talked to him day after day.
- She took advantage of a situation where she found herself alone with Joseph and grabbed him and propositioned him.
- When Joseph turned her down, she covered her tracks by falsely accusing him of approaching her.
- She lied about his intentions and his actions to her staff and to her husband.
- She used the cloak, left behind as a defensive move by Joseph, as her weapon to charge him with adultery.
- She called Joseph a "Hebrew slave" and said his motives were to make sport of her.

Joseph
- He was bought as a slave by Potiphar—an Egyptian and the captain of the guard under Pharaoh.
- Even though he was a slave, the Lord was with Joseph and he prospered.

- He lived in Potiphar's house.
- Potiphar saw that the Lord was with Joseph and put him in charge of his household.
- Because of Joseph, Potiphar's household and everything Joseph was in charge of, and even that which he wasn't, was blessed by the Lord.
- He was wrongly imprisoned.
- Even in prison he flourished because of his relationship with the Lord, who gave him the favor of the warden.

Joseph's Help
- He held a position of trust with his employer.
- He was close to the Lord.

Leader tip: You may want to think about splitting up couples' groups into men's groups and women's groups so that they are able to be more open and honest in their answers for the rest of the questions in this particular session.

With the expanded definition of the commandment in mind, how do you see people "committing adultery" today? What are the results?

Leader note: Have your group think about all of the areas where lust, affairs, and immoral behavior occur and the consequences of giving in to the temptations they present.

Commentary: With the Internet and other electronic devices making communication easier, emotional affairs are on the rise. The availability of pornography is staggering, and everyone is able to secretly obtain it. There is no need to go to the liquor store and be witnessed buying a magazine; anyone, including children, can search for sites and have it available instantly. You can even access pornography on your phone! Virtual reality worlds exist on the Internet where people can make themselves anyone they want to be. They can meet other people in these created worlds and have relationships with them, all under the guise of "it's not real, so it's OK." However, the effects to the human psyche and the damage to relationships are real.

The workplace can present an opportune place for lustful relationships. A husband or wife who isn't happy at home sees someone of the opposite sex in the office who seems a little more put together and a little less needy than their spouse and they have lust in their heart. This only creates more of a chasm in their relationship at home.

Think of "guys' night out" or "girls' night out" and the prospects that might provide for illicit behavior.

Leader tip: Make sure you include those in committed monogamous relationships as well as marriages to underscore the importance of commitment and trust in relationships.

■ **What helps people to *not* give in to the temptation, but flee from it instead?**

Commentary: As in the passage, the trust of someone in a relationship often keeps people from straying and instead can lead them to flee from temptation. Just the idea of hurting someone who loves and trusts them keeps some from indulging in immoral behavior. Others, who are people of integrity, just want to keep their word. Still others may not want to deal with the consequences that would certainly come about if they gave in.

What are some practical steps you can take to safeguard your marriage or relationship and flee when tempted?

Leader note: Talk with your group about boundaries you can set up to help ensure temptations are minimal. Look at what kind of situations should be avoided because immoral opportunities are rampant. Also be sure to focus on keeping existing relationships and marriages healthy. Invest in your marriage by putting in time and effort to make each other happy and fulfilled, thereby eliminating the "need" to look elsewhere.

Leader tip: Remember to consider having men and women separated for this question to allow for more honest and intimate answers. This will help avoid the safe and surface answers and help your group to go deeper and address real issues within relationships.

■ CHAPTER 3: TAKE THAT

■ Did you ever steal something growing up? Did you get caught?

Leader note: It is always a good idea to model this question. Most people, even in the smallest way, have stolen something before. As always, make this as fun as possible. This is not a time to make people feel bad for what they did, just to laugh a little at our mischievousness.

Leader tip: Try to keep stories short or limit the number of people who share to keep this section of the study to five minutes.

▍ What all was involved in Jacob and Rebekah stealing Esau's birthright and blessing?

Leader note: Although everything revolved around deception and manipulation to steal the birthright and blessing, it is most helpful to go through the step-by-step process to get the full magnitude of their actions.

Commentary:

Birthright

- Jacob waited until an opportune time to manipulate the birthright away from his older brother.
- Esau was exhausted and hungry and wanted some stew, so Jacob traded food for the birthright.

Blessing

- Rebekah overheard Isaac tell Esau one evening that he was going to give him the blessing.
- Rebekah told Jacob to get a goat so that she could make a stew for Isaac and make him believe Esau had made it.
- Rebekah and Jacob worked up a disguise so Jacob would appear like Esau to his blind father.
- Rebekah cooked the meal, got Esau's favorite clothes for Jacob to wear, covered Jacob with the goat's fur to make him feel hairier, made fresh bread, and gave the meal to Jacob to give to his father.
- Jacob took the meal to his father and lied about who he was.
- Jacob lied about how he came to have the food so quickly, even invoking the Lord into his scheme.
- Isaac was skeptical and asked to touch the son to make sure which one it was—the hairiness of the goat skin fooled him into believing it was Esau.

- Jacob lied one more time, assuring his father he was really Esau.
- Isaac ate the food and then asked to hug his son to further convince himself it was Esau by smelling his clothes—he was convinced.
- Jacob received the blessing from his father.

■ What were the results?

Commentary:

- Esau traded away his birthright.
- Esau returned from hunting and prepared his father's favorite meal the night he was to receive the blessing.
- When he took the meal to Isaac, his father asked which son it was.
- Esau identified himself and learned that his younger brother had stolen his blessing.
- Jacob received the blessing from his father, which included being served by his brothers.
- Esau wanted another blessing.
- Esau's blessing was one of service to his brother and that of having to fight his way through life; however, he could break free from his brother when he deemed so.
- Esau hated his brother.
- Esau schemed to kill his brother.

■ What are ways, even the most subtle, that people "steal" today? What are the results (both good and bad)?

Leader note: Because "success at any price" is a mantra the world supports, oftentimes stealing becomes part of the game plan. Sometimes the "stealing" is passed off as cheating, or deceit, or manipulation—but whatever you call it, when you end up with something that is not rightfully yours, it is stealing.

Commentary: Consider someone who is deceitful and manipulative and gets the job someone else deserved and worked for honestly. Think about elections where the controlling parties manipulate the outcome with voter fraud. Kids cheat on homework and tests; athletes steal victory when they use performance-enhancing drugs and other unethical means to win; people steal from employers when they take time from their jobs for personal business; family members steal from each other when they are selfish in their actions.

■ **In what areas of your life are you "stealing," and from whom are you "stealing"?**

Leader note: Have your group consider the subtleties discussed in the previous question and see if they relate to any of those answers or if there are other examples that hit closer to home. Think of all aspects of their lives—for example, work, family, church, school, service. Most likely you won't have anyone confess to stealing money or goods, but you may find that your group struggles with other areas of "stealing" that can harm them emotionally and relationally. Try to focus on that type of stealing for these questions.

■ **How does the fact that you are breaking the commandment "You must not steal" affect how you feel about it?**

Leader note: Most people don't consider taking a sick day away from the office to play golf as stealing and especially don't consider it to be breaking one of God's commandments. When they stop and think about it in that way, it may make them reconsider the next time they think about doing it.

■ **What lesson will you take away from this week's study, and how will it change your actions?**

Leader note: You may want to ask this and have them answer silently in prayer at the end of your time together.

■ CHAPTER 4: SHADES OF GREY

■ **Play a round of Two Truths and a Lie and have people try to guess the lie.**

Leader note: Go around the circle and have each group member tell a series of statements about themselves, two statements being true and one being false. Have the rest of the group guess which is the false statement. Remember to only spend about five minutes on this section.

■ **What do you learn about those who keep their word and those who deceive?**

Leader note: You may want to list the characters in the story and write down their actions and consequences to see both the big picture and the details of each account.

All Believers

- They were united in heart and mind.
- They shared all they had because they believed it wasn't theirs to begin with.
- The disciples testified powerfully about Jesus.
- God's blessing was on them.

Joseph (Barnabas)

- He gave all he received for the sale of his property.
- Needs of the people were met.
- There were no needy in the community.

Ananias

- He sold his property but kept some of the money and gave only a portion to the apostles.
- He claimed the amount he gave was the full amount he received for the sale.
- He could have kept the property—there was no reason to lie.
- He lied to the Spirit and to God, not just to men.
- He died on the spot.

Sapphira

- She consented to her husband's lie.
- She conspired with her husband to test the Holy Spirit.
- The last words she heard were that her husband had been carried out dead and she would be too.
- Like her husband, she died on the spot.

What are ways (no matter how subtle) people deceive others today? Why do people deceive others?

Commentary: Little white lies, or gray areas, are ways we describe lying to make it less important, or more acceptable. But in reality, lying is lying—whether white, gray, or any other color.

Sometimes people lie for the fun of it. Others lie to keep themselves out of trouble or to protect themselves. Sometimes people lie to get ahead—they make themselves seem bigger and better than they really are. It could be motivated by trying to get a job, a date, or a loan.

What happens when someone keeps their word? What are the results when they don't?

Commentary: When someone has the reputation of being honest, they gain respect from others. They are deemed trustworthy, and others are able to be more open and intimate with them. When someone lies or is deceitful, they can't be trusted. They alienate friends and family and ultimately lose relationship with others, and with God.

In what areas of your life do you find it easy to keep your word, and in what areas are you deceitful, even in the most subtle ways?

Leader note: Your group will probably share the subtle ways they stretch the truth, tell white lies, and withhold information rather than confess major lies and deceptive ways. Don't push the subject too much but consider holding a time of prayer at the end when people can confess offenses that they didn't feel comfortable sharing in a group setting.

When you consider that even little white lies are breaking the commandment, how does that affect what you'll say going forward?

Leader note: Most people consider white lies as a way of protecting others or themselves and don't consider it as breaking one of God's commandments. When they take the time to think about it, they may change how easily they move toward deceit when presented with a tough situation.

▄▄▄ CHAPTER 5: MINE!

■ What is something you don't have that you would love to get?

Leader tip: Spend only about five minutes on this question.

Leader note: This should be a fun and easy question for your group to answer. There are always new gadgets on the market that people want to get, or maybe a new car. Just keep the conversation light, as we will be delving into a more emotional study following this question.

■ What are the ways King Ahab and Jezebel coveted, and what were the results?

Commentary:
- Ahab wanted the property next to his palace that belonged to his neighbor Naboth.
- He offered to trade for it or purchase it outright.
- The neighbor wouldn't sell it because of his direction from the Lord to not do so.
- Ahab was angry, pouted, and went to bed without dinner.
- Jezebel reminded Ahab he was the king and could have anything he wanted.
- Jezebel told Ahab she would handle it.
- Jezebel forged letters in her husband's name and commanded the leaders and elders to arrange for the murder of Naboth.
- The murder was executed just as Jezebel commanded.
- Ahab went to claim the property of Naboth.

- Elijah met Ahab at the site of the vineyard and delivered the message from the Lord that God was angry with Ahab for murdering Naboth and claiming his land.
- Ahab heard that he and all male descendants would have disaster brought on them.
- God said Ahab had led Israel to sin through his actions.
- Ahab learned Jezebel would die right where his covetousness began.

What is the difference between desire and coveting? What makes people move from having a healthy desire to coveting?

Leader note: *Desire* is defined as "to wish or long for." *Covet* is defined as "to desire wrongfully, inordinately, or without due regard for the rights of others."

Leader note: Before giving the definitions to your group, ask them to try to explain the difference between *desire* and *covet*. Then give them the definitions.

Commentary: The quickest road from desire to covet goes right through discontentment. If people are not content with their place in life, their own possessions, their job, their family, and so forth, they begin looking elsewhere and the coveting begins. It is emotionally impossible to be content and covetous at the same time.

Where in your life do you struggle with keeping your desires in check?

Leader note: You may want to answer this question first to provide a safe place for disclosure.

Commentary: Most people struggle in at least one area of their life due to dissatisfaction with their own circumstances. It may be your body, house, job, toys, position, relationships, or something completely different, but most people have something they border on coveting.

■ **If you have coveted in the past (or struggle with it now), how does it affect your life?**

Commentary: This goes hand in hand with the previous question. What were the results of something you coveted in the past, and how can you learn from those results and apply it to what you are coveting now? How did it affect your attitude, your joy in life? Did it affect you physically, as it did Ahab? Did you turn bitter or even become manipulative to gain what you wanted?

■ **What are some practical steps you can take to keep from coveting?**

Leader note: Consider ways to be more grateful for what you have and who you are. Maybe it is through serving those who are in need. It could be you need to make a list of things for which you are grateful and pray a prayer of thanksgiving every day for those things. Maybe you need to be happy for and compliment others on those very things you tend to covet— their car, their home, their new job, their new boat, and so on. When you are sincerely happy for others, it is much more difficult to covet their circumstances or things.

LIQUID would love to thank:

Chris Marcus, for being a producer, designer, editor, and director of photography on the project. You did it all, and we could not have done it without you.

Mariners Church: To the staff and small group department, for all of their help and insight into this entire project. And to the congregation and elder board for their prayers and support.

Kenton Beshore, for the beauty of flow questions.

All of the incredible people in North Carolina, who got this whole thing started.

The cast and crew, for the endless hours of hard work and incredible performances.

Aaron and Mark of Tank Creative, for making us sound good.

Chris Ferebee of Yates and Yates, for all of his guidance and direction.

Cindy Western, for her help in crafting great questions.

Our incredible editor, Kim Hearon, who, to put it simply, had to deal with us. You made it fun.

Sunny Stam, for the amazing photography.

All the people at Thomas Nelson, for your hard work and expertise.

And we thank God for having his hand on this project and blessing it.